You Can Talk to God

by Sara Awad

Illustrated by Penny Webber

TO

_____

FROM

_____

DATE

_____

You Can Talk to God

With deepest gratitude to Reverend Lisa Carson for all her guidance and support.

Dear parents and teachers,

I am excited to share this little book with you and your children. As a licensed Religious Science practitioner and ministerial student, I know firsthand the power of prayer in general and affirmative prayer in particular. In this work, I have taken the five steps of treatment and presented them in a simple, easy-to-follow way that even the youngest child can readily understand. As Dr. Ernest Holmes taught us, we have the power to realize the presence of the divine in every moment, and in doing so, we can create experiences of wholeness.

Once children know that everything they perceive in the outer world with their five senses is a creation of their own thoughts, ideas, and beliefs, they can begin to use affirmative prayer treatment with power and intention. And in so doing, they can use their words to bring greater love, joy, harmony, and abundance into their young lives. What I offer children with this book is a step-by-step guide to effective prayer treatment and the understanding that all they could ever want or need is already within them, just waiting to be recognized.

It is my belief that as children become more confident and skilled travelers on the inward path, they become more deeply attuned to the reality of good that is always present and develop a solid foundation of spiritual practice that will serve them throughout their lives. I have included blank workbook pages at the end of the book to be used for practice in writing prayer treatments, as well as a question-and-answer section. My wish is that each child comes to know the unlimited power and presence of Universal Spirit as the ultimate reality and the true nature of who and what they are.

Sara Awad, RScP

Prayer is how we connect with our higher selves,
Some people call this part of themselves God

You can talk to God
anytime, any day,
by using your words
in a special way.

You don't have to be frightened
or ask for something small.
If it does no harm,
you can have it all!

3

the wisdom that lives within us.
or Spirit or Universal Mind or even Source.

You can call it whatever feels best for you.

In our teaching we say a special kind of prayer.

It's called affirmative prayer.
Keep reading to learn the five steps of treatment!

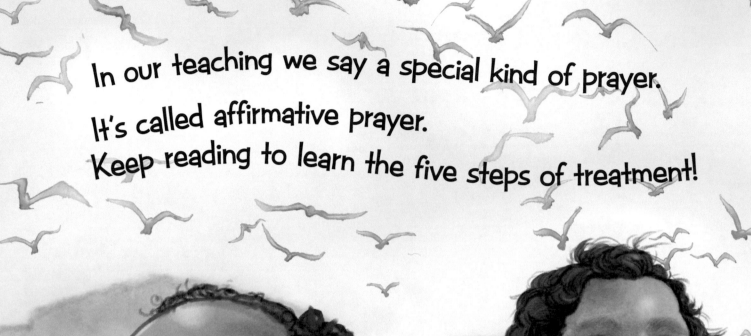

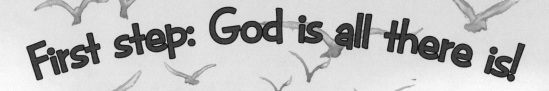

First step: God is all there is!

God is in everything;
there is nowhere it's not.
It's in you and in me
and in every spot.

It's the only power
and the only source.
It is generous and kind
and loving, of course.

God is everywhere.
   When we remember this,
we know **we are never alone.**

6

Second step: I am one with God!

God is not separate;
it's part of you.
It's all that you are
and all that you do.

7

God lives in me, and I live in God.
We are one.

It's the part of you
that smiles and dances and sings—
the part of you that's helpful
and shares your things.

Third step: I claim my good!

When you speak your word
and you trust that's its true,
then blessings will flow
in abundance to you!

Even when everything
looks like a mess,
there's an invisible power
that wants to express.

Even when you are worried or afraid, the
wisdom in you always knows what to do.

Step four: I give thanks!

Köszi

When you say thank you
each time you pray,
it multiplies your abundance
in every way.

Grazie

Gracias

11

Step five: I let go and let God!

I let it all go,
and I let it all be,
trusting in God
to take care of me.

I don't have to wonder.
I don't have to guess.
When I speak my word,
God only says yes!

It is

And so it is!
is what you can say
to finish your treatment
each time you pray.

done!

Treat and move your feet!

TREATMENT IS A SPECIAL WORD FOR PRAYER.

You've said your prayers;
now what should you do?
You can listen to
what God says to you.

Listen to your mind;
listen to your heart.
And they will show you
how to do your part.

You can ask yourself, what is mine to do?

YOU ARE GOD
IN ACTION.

My First Prayer Treatment

1. God Is _____

_____

2. I Am _____

_____

3. I Claim My Good _____

_____

4. I Give Thanks _____

_____

5. I Let Go And Let God _____

_____

And So It Is!

There is nothing between us and God but our own thoughts and beliefs.
—Ernest Holmes

Questions

The following pages have questions for parents and teachers relating to the material presented. You can share these questions with your children or students to help them cultivate a deeper understanding of spiritual principles related to affirmative prayer.

When it's hard to believe. All of us have times when we feel so sad or scared or mad that it isn't easy to remember that God is right where we are. When that happens, we can take as much time as we need to remind ourselves. Can you think of a time when you felt mad or sad, but you remembered God's good was everywhere and things turned out better then you thought?

When things look or feel bad. Sometimes things break, or we get hurt or sick. Those things are real, and we don't have to pretend that they aren't. All we have to do is remember that wherever the problem is, God is too. When we remember God's wholeness is everywhere, things get better. What is one thing that you would like to remember the truth about?

When I don't know what to pray for. Sometimes we know exactly what we want to pray about, but other times we don't. That's OK! We can just pray for the highest and best good, and the right things will happen. Sometimes God comes up with ideas that are even better than our own. Can you think of a time when you didn't know what to pray for, but God still provided exactly what you needed?

When you aren't sure what words to say. When we pray, our feelings are more important than our words. You don't have to worry about what words to choose. You can use the ones you know. What matters is that you feel it in your heart. Love has a feeling. So does abundance and peace. What do those things feel like to you?

When you pray and nothing happens. We have all had times when it seems like our prayers are not being answered. Of course they are! God always answers, but it only gives us what we believe will happen. Can you think of a time when you prayed for something, but you didn't really think it was possible or you didn't think you deserved it? Sometimes it helps to start by asking for things one piece at a time so that it's easier for you to imagine. As you bless and take joy in each small step, your faith in God will grow, and so will your good.

If you don't like the word God. It doesn't matter whether you call your higher self God, Spirit, Source, Universal Presence or anything else. What's important is that you know that it is part of you and you are part of it. When we pray, we are really just turning within and talking to the part of us that always knows what is best.

Balboa Press books may be ordered through booksellers or by contacting:

Balboa Press
A Division of Hay House
1663 Liberty Drive
Bloomington, IN 47403
www.balboapress.com
844-682-1282

Because of the dynamic nature of the Internet, any web addresses or links contained in this book may have changed since publication and may no longer be valid. The views expressed in this work are solely those of the author and do not necessarily reflect the views of the publisher, and the publisher hereby disclaims any responsibility for them.

ISBN: 979-8-7652-2648-3 (sc)
ISBN: 979-8-7652-2649-0 (e)

Print information available on the last page.

Balboa Press rev. date: 03/25/2022

Printed in the United States
by Baker & Taylor Publisher Services